The Way of Love
and Peace

The Way of Love and Peace

Adam F Jones

authorHOUSE®

AuthorHouse™
1663 Liberty Drive
Bloomington, IN 47403
www.authorhouse.com
Phone: 1-800-839-8640

First published by AuthorHouse   08/17/2011

ISBN: 978-1-4567-8948-0 (sc)
ISBN: 978-1-4567-8947-3 (ebk)

Printed in the United States of America

This book is printed on acid-free paper.

Parable Nature

A parable nature is a lot of fun;
It is about the moon and the sun.
Which one is best for lighting our world?

I believe the moon, for lighting up the night sky
Yet when the sun rises in the east and sets in the west,
There is no greater flame in heaven.

Where are the little ones to read my work?

The Workable Art

Where in the world did I find my mind?
I found it in the beauty of nature,
In the three dimensional world.

How do I perceive the work of nature?
To be workable art.
How do I perceive the workable art?
To be workable reality in its self.

Immortality

In the ancient past God would have been
A child uncloth'd in the realm of time.A naked child in the
kingdom of life
Who are the teachers of immortality?
The child in our arm
Where is the arm of immortality?

Inside our very heart.

Culture

In laws of past cultures,
Culture was considered to be law.
In our law, culture is obsolete
In truth, there should be a world of love for your mind.

A web of love is the culture of love,
A system without border or boundary.
How many living forms exist in our system?
Only one can survive.

How many people believe in love?

The Smallest Form

The smallest of form
Gave birth to the greatest love
In the universe.

I searched for the truth
And found only 'I'am'.
In my heart I sought to consume
My very human form,
To dissolve into nothing.
I found something greater than love,
Greater than freedom:

The very honour of the all.

Big Bang

In the beginning there was no Big Bang,
But a tear of energy that expanded and folded
A silent vehicle of our measure.

Do you understand gravity?
It is not about mass but dust,
Harnessing the secret energy of dust.

Why do I speak of such things?
Because I am gravitational.

How do you see yourself in millennia?
I see you in our realm.

The Teacher

There is nothing a woman cannot do or achieve,
Nothing she cannot be;
She has only one rule left:
Not to be superior to man himself.

A man can achieve almost anything
But can he achieve the very thing
He desires the most, peace?

A child can achieve almost immortality
When I am their very teacher.

Abaddon

He was forsaken by his father,
Left to die by his mother,
Naked, alone and crying for his law

Abaddon is not real;
He is as all human beings are.
The law of nature,
The law of life.

Bed Of Happiness

My love and affection is warning you
I have nothing left but contempt.
Where did I find my humour?
I found it in my loneliness.
How much longer shall I smile,
Knowing we will never meet?

I'm sure we will meet one day;
In a bed of happiness we shall sleep together,
Our hearts are pure, and we will ask why

God does not sleep or wake.

The Whole Body

Where did I find myself in the world?
I found myself in your heart.
Where did I find my love?
In your heart,

How do I comprehend the love I found?
In the pilgrimage for the whole body,
I found the heart to be the truth.

God does not sleep or wake.

The Law Of Nature

I am unpopular and popular,
Ridiculed and praised.

I hide in all bodies, I live in all forms;
I have seen a thousand times my size,
A thousand times my demise.

I have exalted and condemned
Cherished and neglected
I 'am the enemy and the friend
Nature and beyond nature
Natural and unnatural
I 'am Celestial and mortal

I 'am the law of nature
I 'am the law of life

Design

There isn't a law that will not cause troubled hearts
A law that will not cause troubled minds

A Holy book or scripture that will not cause distress
Or enlighten the mind
There is an origin for everything in humankind
Why did God create the world in seven days?
Sight, sound, taste and smell
The reality of the senses
Do my words touch your heart?

It was not a prophecy; It was a design

For man to be a prophet of God for mankind

Who are we talking to in our mind,
When we desire not truth but design?

Paradise

How should we talk about the nature of our being?
I talk through parables for the world to be real.

'In paradise you shall see rivers of milk and honey,
In paradise you will know
The light reflects a river of milk,
A pathway of honey that leads to the sun.

Love For Truth

In space there is only emptiness.
We fill it with our love for truth,
A tear of our human joy
Do we fear emptiness?
Do we fear the loss of a child?

There will be no more for me after
I have spoken for the last time.
How do I compare to a newborn babe

Do I compare?

I 'Am God

Why are they talking about time?
The time is not now;
It is only ever now.
I say it because I am the truth.
I repeat it because I' am a creature of love

I talk about the thing I am,
The law of life
The law of loving people

I m greater than any animal;
I am a human being
I am a God

Lion Thumb

Did we find our soul in the hand of an animal?
You, my friend, are an animal, too.

Hold out your hand and tell me,
How many fingers do you have?
Five is not the answer—it is four.

How do I know this to be truthful?
I have a thumb no bigger than a lion's thumb.

Who took the thorn out of the lion's paw?
You have been chosen to be my lion.

Do you like my humour?
I like my lion raw.

Love is not for us to play with;
Love is for us to experience.

Way Of Nature

Where in the world do we find our law?
I found my law in the way of nature
It is the way of seeing and believing,
Knowing and understanding,
Logic and reason.

A very open law, indeed

Heart Of God

There isn't a heart in the heart of a God;
Only a whole sword.
It is very unique,
It does not fight you,
It does not harm you or unnerve you.

I call it a whole sword,
A complete weapon.
Who shall raise their hand to me?
Only the one who carries a weapon!

Armoury

How many holding arms
Sit in my armoury?
I have no idea how many.
Pull me another one,
Pull me another two.

How many holding arms
Sit in my armoury now?
They are empty—
Why is this so?

There isn't an armoury
That can conquer our law.

Theatre Of Warfare

Give up your soul to me,
Give up your heart to my arm.
How much is it to buy my arm from you?
You may ask me why!

I ask you for my heart.
How much can I offer for your soul?
Is it for sale?

How much can I bargain with you?
For sale, no sale.

How much can I beg you for your arm?
I beg you for an arm sale to me;
Now I am calling the bargain.
How many people are in my theatre of warfare?

The Arm

How did I know you knew?
Why did you know I left you to know?
How did I Knew? ?
I know I say it incorrectly.
How did I know you knew it?

What am I doing with this question?
It is I who knows why I say it.
Let me hold you in my arms;
I am held to in the arms of someone else.
Whose arm can this be?
I could only dream it is you.

Why is this a dream?
Because we are like children in truth:
As vast as it isn't,
We just play with our dreams,
And that's all I really believe.
How do I believe in your dream?

I hope it is for me too.

A New Order

In the beginning parable

We were inside ourselves,
Inside our being;
We were never here for anything
Other than a new order,
An order of life and law.

Are you aware of life?
I am not aware of life yet.
Our law is simple—it is called
'You are our law'.

Solitary Character

I am happy, happier than I've ever been.
Inside my heart, there is a solitary character
Who tells a tale of solitude!
The Romance of the heart

I found it in my mindIn my whole life.
I saw solitude to be the truth
I haven't lived enough to know the truth

.

In solitude there is one simple law
To seek the love of truthThe romance of the Heart

Gentleness

How do I see the truth in you,
I see it in your fingers, in your soul.

How do you write with your fingers?
We use our souls to write with our fingers.
Our love to write with our arm is final.
Final destination is not what I am.
Insidious people write with their arm;
Gentle people write with their hand.

I am a human being who has attacked with his arm.
I am most certainly cowardly,

How do I redeem myself?
I must speak the truth:
All anger of the arm,
Be this physical or written,
Is most certainly an ideology of mental habits!

Condition

In the world there are troublesome minds.
How lucky I am to be me;
How unfortunate I am to be troubled.

Inside my brain I have a condition called
Psychosis and the symptoms of schizophrenia
It harms my life and ruins my dreams.
The way I see and feel the world is strange.

How many voices are there in my mind?
Not as many as you think.
Why do I tell the truth?
I believe I behold the reality.

That's my condition in all of my dreams.

God Or Devil

Do we believe in the Devil?
It isn't real, and for a reason
It is not real.

How do we create a demon?
We conjure up the creatures of nature,
Swirl them into a monster,
And create a demon.

What makes us jump back?
When we see a demon or Satan,
Give it the voice of a lion,And you will be fearful and afraid

How do we create a God?
Conjure up the creatures of nature,
Swirl them into a God.
What makes us draw near?
It is in our nature to be a god.

How do I create a God for you? ?
Conjure up your own soul.
Be pure and live longer.
Be impure and live shorter lives.

Purity

I believe in something called purity.
I know purity is real.

How do I feel when I say this?
I feel anger
Inside our genes.
There are infinite switches;
They switch often enough
From purity to impurity.
Perfection to imperfection

How do I choose purity?
I know the law of nature dictates.
Whatever you put into your body
May one day condemn you!

Perfectly Balanced

Perfection will not condemn you.
The love of perfection
Will not condemn you.
Where are your friends in life right now?

Living perfect lives in this perfect realm.
Do you see perfection in the universe?
It is perfectly balanced.

One World

How long are the roads in our minds?
Longer than the whole world.
How long is a piece of string?

We live in a quantum reality
Therefore I cannot tell you.

How many worlds are there within a world?
I believe in only one world

Because it is impossible to live
In a different world than our world.

Sign Language

How many times are there in a thousand times?
This is a conundrum.
How many times are there in a thousand years?
Do the mathematical calculation, and reap the reward.

There is no reward in times; only ages are rewarding.
How do I perceive the ages?
I think about culture.

What are signs for in ages?
They're there for hypocritical thinking.
How do I say this without being a hypocrite myself?
Because I love sign language and people.

Knowledge

Love isn't love I know it isn't
Because I know love is difficult.
For the human being of knowledge,
It is painful to see love.

When we are looking for an answer,
We see suffering all the time.
Without knowledge we say
Suffering cannot be conquered.

I know this is hard to suffice:
I shall wait for you
To love me too?

The Illusion

There is a code of conduct
The way of nature:
It isn't evil, it is truthful;
It isn't harmful, it is truthful to.

It knows no bounds and owns no souls.

In fact it is an illusion.
It hurts those who indulge it;
It is called suffering.

Will we ever be free?
I believe one day we will be pure,
Our hearts will be happy,
We will be free of unhappiness.

How do I feel inside?
Sometimes like a soul betrayed
With the kiss of poison.
I have poisoned my soul
With the indulgence of poison.

Sahara Desert

I am here for a reason.
What reason do I choose?
Loving you is my reason,
Choosing you, too.

How many water holes are therein the Sahara desert?
I can name only one.
My hole is bigger than your hole.
How many holes are there in the desert?
Why the desert?
Where are our starry skies!

Poverty

There is a well of light inside the mind.
Are we the poorest of humankind?
I am immensely happy for human life.

The mind wanders vast plains
Looking for something to drink,
And nourishment too.
How does the brain know I am lying?
Lying to myself always—

I see truthful people lying to me.
How do we make poverty history?
I believe we should be honest.

Poverty does not exist inside the human body;
It exists only in the physical world,
Inanimate infrastructure.

Holy One

Who is the holy one ?
When I know something,
I question my honesty;
When I see something,
Question my integrity.

Where do we come from?
The loving one—
I am here to question the loving one too,

Here to question the power, and the glory

Here to question his law
The holy one is not beyond question
The loving one is holy.

Realm Of Species

There is a story I have to tell
There is a baby of great joy in my arm.
It is non-human in form
And human in form, too.
It does not exist in the realm of reality.

It is exists in the realm of our species,
A human being.
There are no laws in our realm;
There is only being human.

Life will not accept us in the universe
If we are non-human in form.

Field Reeds

Let us love our work.
It is I and you—
We are workable art,
Nature's field of reeds.

Have you seen a field of reeds?
We are human beings;
It is for us to believe
We are all equal.

One Organic Life

In the beginning
We were one organic life.

I offered my body as the human form,
The human form as my being,
The human being as my mind.

Love does not offer itself to love,
Power to power,
Knowledge to knowledge.
It offers itself to none.

We are very blessed,
Loved in all we do.

Believe

I need you to love more than you love,
To think more than you think,
To believe more than you believe.
Who am I?
I am he who does not believe in himself.
I am she who does not believe in herself.

I am in love with my very law.

Knowledge Of Purity

Parables are the knowledge of purity;
They are the reality of our dimension.
Where in the world do you find a parable?

In the layers of a onion,
In the depths of our souls,

We find them hidden in our realm,
In our very secret cave.
No greater than a star are our parables.

Tale Of Two Stones

There is a tale I have not told you,
The tale of two stones.

They are precious stones indeed.
One stone is called 'I am',
The other stone is you.

Who said you are not loved, my friend
Would you like to throw this stone and cast me down?

I offer you two stones and two choices.
The first choice is I die.
The second choice is you live.
How many of those choices do you desire?

Intelligence

Stop pretending you have won
And pretend you have lost instead.
How many intellects does it take to capture
An intelligent man?

How many intelligent women
Does it take to hold onto an intelligent woman?
Be careful of intelligence it may be flawed.

Altruism dictates when fear is aroused;
Intelligence becomes dominant.

I know it does; I see it for real reasons:
Men and women confusing there reality
For reasons I myself do not know.

The Sea

I have a way I call the mind's process

How many shells are there in the sea?
How many stars are there in the sky?
How many worlds are there in the universe?

Why I have become so repetitive?
I see the human soul in every star,
The body in every shell.
How many shells are there in the sea?
So many I can barely believe

Tree Of Life

How many species can we fit in the Tree of Life?
Nature can fit, only as many as suffice

How many lovable people
Does it take to honour a law of love?

More people than it takes species,
More feeling than any creature to love.
How many kingdoms are in your mind?
Only one kingdom will suffice
How many human beings
See the world through two eyes?

Many see the world do they see the whirlwind
Not unless they see with two eyes.

Resting With You

Let yourself rest; I'm resting with you.
Let yourself argue with yourself;
I'm at rest with you.

I am aware of you all the time,
Like a mother watching from the corner of her eye,
Like a father who knows he is secure.

Do you believe nature to be a violent being?
Nature is a natural organism,
Herself, himself
Nature isn't a violent human being
A non-violent human being
Nature is God

A Human Being

I am who you think I am,
A Human being, and for a reason
I live for you!

How many times have I seen you in life?
I have so many eyes,
I see everything all of the time
How many forms see?
I 'am blinded by the light

Little Human Beings

How many are the ones who love?
So many I believe in their souls.
The little human being is my friend.
Would you dare lay a finger on a little human being?

Who are these little human beings?
They are the future of human life
Do you remember being small enough
To dream of great celestial beings
I remember being uncloth'd;
We were free from our souls.

Who is it we are talking to
In this very immortal home?

We are like children talking to
Our imaginary friend.

Holy Lands

How many holy lands are there in the universe?
I can name only two; there are many more.

How many human beings question a holy land?
In what direction should we pray?

We seek truth and freedom.
To live in a perfect universe.

There is no holy land
In the world of our ancient ancestor,
No place on earth that is a fixed point.
The sun is the fixed point of our solar system,
Yet the universe is ever expanding.

Sphinx

There was child who became a lion,
A guardian of the three-dimensional world.
Sphinx was his name,
Posture, strength and awareness his dream.
A dream about a star,
A resurrection star.
Why did the dream fail??
Fixed in his place,
Never to be reborn again.

What is the meaning of this story?
It is about water and spirit:
It never ceases to flow and change.

Like the air we breathe,
Breath and water.

Resurrection

How do we contemplate ourselves all the time?
When we are impossibly wrong
To put our trust in our own work,
Do you think there will be resurrection?
It has already happened in the realm of digital code—
Quantum mechanical altruism;
The Great workable art is real.

Yet there is a warning:
Where are the minds in these digital forms?
They are our mind.

Resurrection is for us to experience,
Not for us to recreate.

The Powerful Friend

There is no arm in our armoury;
There is only a place for an armoury.

Who are the real warriors?
They are inside our mind.
I have so many I can barely function.
They're trying to spin a web of fictitious dreams.
How do I know my language is right?

I have barely begun to dream about my powerful friend;
I believe him to be a poet
And a loving being.

Friends

How do we perceive the holy ones?
How do we embrace the unholy ones?

I see them as friends,

Because I am troubled
By my friend, the enemy.
How much time can I spend in my own company?

Not enough time to love the world.
I love dearly.

The Silence

How old were you when a family member died?
It is not real to people, death.

We become recycled organic matter,
But there is something else that concerns me.
It is not God or the devil;
It is someone called a human being.

How do I perceive nature?
I feel you but cannot see you;
I feel fear and see suffering
Even if I cannot see
That's what concerns me.

I believe there is something
I call greatness.
I feel, hear, but cannot see.
What is it I love about the true cost of words?
It isn't truthful to talk.

The Law Of Mankind

Pleasure is the law of mankind.
We cannot find peace in pleasure;
The whole system induces conflict.

Who sees conflict?
The one who sees all
Sees everything we do
In the world of humankind,

There isn't a saying that does not proclaim,
'I am the law your father never knew,
The life your mother never observed.'

There is a saying in our language, too:
Whoever dares to challenge the law of life
Shall not succeed.

I Saw You

I saw you as a human being.
You were naked in my home;
Your beauty is the cause of my sin,
Your body my holiness.

I saw you as a child,
A woman,
A man.

How do I see you now?
A child in my arms.

Noah's Ark

There is a story of a man
Who lived for a thousand years!
He built a vessel called the ark.

I have a vessel for you to behold:
It is called the human form.
How many animals have I consumed?
More than on the ark.
How many have I protected?
Only one.

The Beautiful World

There is a woman who sowed a fieldThe field is called the
beautiful world.
She tosses the grain into the field
And reaps a wonderful reward.

There is only one problem:
The field is not her own.
There is a terrible storm on the horizon.
She collects as much as she can;
The storm destroys the rest of the crop.

It is called the parable of the world.

Bread Of Heaven

The triune mind is not real
Because there is no cold blood in human life,
I have indeed resurrected
The bread of my ancient ancestor.

How do I discuss their being,
Knowing their end could be mine,
Knowing I could become extinct?

I feel a sense of wonder
Knowing organic life was
Evolving form after form
To avoid its own extinction.

I live inside this bread of heaven,
The very bone of your body.
I am engineering my own extinction
For a reason I cannot tell you.

Cycles

How many cycles have there been?
As many as you have seen.
I believe in a cycle of time
Evolving around the sun.

We are here to be crowned
With the procession of the planets,
To be formed in the stars.
I have been crowned by my friends' will.
I am in love with my friend

The one who has no friends
Is a friend of the world.

Suit Of Love

How many suits do you have?
Only one suit do I wear;
It is called the suit of love.

What do I know about you my friend?
I know you wear a suit of armour.

I will become a flu virus to get to you,
Like the air you breathe!
How do I know this?
I am a little bit cunning.

Voice Of A Messenger

Where is the one that talks to human life?
There is a law I do not understand
The law I call the secret life
I believe in something I call God
It does not talk unless I talk
Am I talking to myself?

I believe I 'am talking to myself
The truth of talking is
To express your fear and redeem your soul

Woman And Man

A woman is in love,
She is in love for him,
In love for herself.
She does not demand of him,
She demands of no one, only herself.

Why do men love women?
Because their faces are united.
Why do women love men?
Because their faces are united
In love and peace.

A woman who loves only a man
Is not a woman of the law!
A man who loves only a woman
Is not a man of the law of love!

Infinite Moments

How many moments are there in a moment?
An hour, a minute, a second.

There are many moments in a second;
Infinite moments have just occurred.

I say a moment is inescapable
Because you experience the moment.

Inescapable.

Joseph Merrick

I am a human being.
Who said these words?
A man chosen by God
From a field of reeds.

They are the words of a man named
Joseph Carey Merrick,
Called the elephant man.He isn't a God of India
I believe Joseph to be the child of Nature
His family are begotten too

Lonely Holy Man

How many times does your heart beat in a millisecond?
A thousand times a second.
Prove me wrong; I know you're right.

The brain beats in tune with the heart.
It beats a solemn tune for a holy man.

I am waiting for my fulfilment,
For my song to explore
It's new found rhythm.

What is the song to be called?
The song of the lonely holy man.
I think you should fall in love
With my rhythm

The Whirlwind

How many times does a whirlwind rotate in a second?
You may know the answer; you may not.

How many times in loneliness
Do you feel a whirlwind of need?
I feel only necessity.

How many times does a black hole rotate?
I'm never alone in my home.

What do you think I am, my friend?
Darker than the dark,
I am lighter than the light.
Crowning you in glory,
With the procession of the planets—
Where in the universe did you find your crown?

The Gateway

How many windows are in your house?
My house has too many windows.

How do you see them in their own right?
I see a window as a gateway.
Gateway to where?
Gateway to our friendship.

How many homes do you need to be free?
In our environment, we need only one environment.
There is no environment in space time.
How do you know I'm telling the truth?
The space-time continuum.

How many windows are in a planetary cycle?
One window of opportunity:
The law of nature.

Information

Information is the beginning of the world.
How do I know it is the end of the world, too?
I have seen information;
It is a heart full of worry,
A tear full of burden.

My loving friend believes
There are one or two ways to die.
The first way to die is to believe in you;
The second way to die
Is to believe in information.

There are laws at my command:
'Thou shall not kill'.
'Thou shall not feel guilty'.

Who among you created an idol?
I believe in idols too
I believe in you

End Of Time

There will be a law for all of time.

It will be for us to know our law,
To see our human souls
It will be for you to see
Male, female, and Love,
Listen to what I teach:
There is no law that has not been
Created by God
There is no life that has not been
Created by nature
Who are we to be the truth?
We are the truth

Conceal Truth

How do we conceal truthfulness?
We conceal our hearts
How do we conceal our hearts?
We conceal our truthfulness
There are One hundred Billion stars
How do we conceal our truthfulness?
When there is only one Kingdom of neurons
Only heaven is as full

Inside our heart we are in the universe
Completely in the universe

Forever and ever is not the truth
It is the reality

Black Hole

A timeless zone is a black hole
How many times will I have to say 'black hole'.

Who is the provider of infant form?
A human being
Who is the provider of power?
The law of nature
I do take offence with destruction.
I believe I am the very law of destruction.
I am a human being,

Violence

I am thinking about a question I need to ask:
What is the meaning of a black hole?

Because we are asked to die
And we refuse;
Because we don't want to die
In a non-violent or violent way.

How do you die for a law?
We die as one body for a reason,
So violent and non-violent death
Are considered a law unto themselves.

Orion

What branch of the tree of life do we sit on?
Are we the descendants of Adam and Eve?
The living man

Did Eve come from the rib of Adam,
Or the constellation Orion?
The living man, the star man

How many virgins are there who have given birth?
Only one.
The living woman, the star woman

What is the nature of our God?
I believe it is called life,
Natural complexity and simplicity.

I Beget Myself

There are many rules that govern the Universe
How many of those rules do we hold in our Hand?
In our kingdom there are no rules to hold in our hand
There are no rules to behold in our heart

How many kingdoms are in your mind?
Only one Kingdom of neurons
Only the way of love
The way of peace
How do I beget myself?

I believe I beget myself

We Will Meet

I am in the throes of your arms,
The joy of your very body,
Kindling a light in your mind,
Dreaming a dream in your very soul.

We will meet in this light;
We will meet one day
You be certain of that

Do you know who my friend is?
My little friend is the truth.

Weaving Web

We are weaving a web around your soul.
Is it for your soul to be caught
In my web of deceit?

How many stars are there in a galaxy?
How many are there above and below?
We may never know.

How many do you have in your suit?
Inside there is another realm,
A complete unity?
Yet there is only one for you.

A star is not a planet.

Heart And Brain

All the time we try to stay awake,
We find ourselves dreaming.
Sometimes I call it the self,
Sometimes the soul.

How do I dream when I am asleep?
I think my heart does the dreaming for me.
Our hearts need our brain;
Our dreams need our hearts.

I dream, too, about you and me,
Where am I in your heart!

Holier Than Warfare

You have turned the house of my father
Into a den of thieves.
What is a house of purity?
A place of deceit,
A place of insecurity.
We have breathed a house of sinfulness,
Lived a life of truthfulness.

We do battle with the devil himself,
Battle with Satan herself.
I have seen no warfare myself,
Nothing but tranquillity.

What is our concern?
Holier than warfare is our concern,
Satisfaction and contentment.

The Ten Commandants

How many members of the family
We are here to dissolve
Have known about the law of love?

There are many rules and laws
That determine a family of four.
Many rules and laws
That determines a family of six.
There are Ten Commandments,
Six to be dissolved.

The first law is to be exalted;
The second law is to be condemned.
Why is this so?
It is a law created by human life.

A Thousand Times

We have broken the law a thousand times,
Broken our will a thousand times too,

How will we ever be free??
I hope we never pray for any law.
Love is about conditioning,
Self-discipline.
How will we know when we are free?
We will feel it inside.

Drawing Up The Light

There are many more who know.
I am not one of those who knows
How much it takes to fend for one's self.

To observe one's own doing
Certainly involve one's own soul.
We draw from the light
Until we tire of drawing up the light;
We become a little darker,
Would like to be settled.

Inside the soul a great whirlpool churns.
It tells you never stop pulling on the rope,
To draw up the essence of the light.

The Real World

We worry about the real world,
About ourselves and the future.

I am certainly simple;
My writing is simple, too.
I 'am complete beyond complexity
And also simple to look at.

It is simple to look at
The natural world—
It is the complexity of it
I find confusing.

Illusion is only for intelligence;
Purity is only for the soul.

Competition

Our origins are further back than we believe.
There are animals in the nature of all human beings;
They cannot accept a non-violent death.

Human beings are competitors,
But how do you measure competition?
Is competition the greatest endeavour?

How do we measure balance?
To be well balanced in body and soul.
Why do I say soul?
I am talking about the human mind.

In a world of men and women of great intelligence,
Genetic beauty and athletic ability,
How do I compete?

What is left to enjoy?
Is it our own human form?
Our own balance our own purity?
But how far must that purity to be pure?

Satisfaction and contentment
Is all purity ever was and will ever be.

Law Of Ideology

What is the nature of the truth in the world?
The law of life.
The truth of the law is to succumb
To your own enemy,
The nature of ideology—
I am the law of ideology, too.

The Garden Of Eden

How many moments are there in time?
As many as you thought.

In time what is the meaning of time?
It is time.
In time what is the meaning of human life?
It is what we do with our time.

There is a sun dial in a garden,
The Garden of Eden.
Sit down beside me and hear these words.

All is shapes and shadows;
Nothing else exists.

Endless Struggle

You are free to be who you choose,
Free to be chosen.
Yes. my dear friend,
How many more shall there be?
As many as the Tree of Life can produce.

It is an endless struggle
For the soul to be free,
The body to be pure.
A law of life,
A law of power,
A law of truthfulness.

Life in the universe!

Celibate Children

I am at war with my own ideology.
I am a man of idol worship.
My idol is Jesus Christ.

Who are the sons and daughters of God?
They are celibate children,
The celestial father and mother's children

I believe celibacy to be genetic.
Why genetic?
We are all genealogy in genes.

I am destined to be in love.
I'm in love with a woman always in my mind.
Could a cave or a monastery change desire?

I think it would be possible to change desire.
As difficult as desire is,
I believe it is possible to be free, too.

Cross Of Intoxication

There is a place called the beginning of nature

How do we begin our evolution inside the womb?
Is it the beating heart that awakes our form?,
Do we become the heart beat?

How do we satisfy our need for food and water?
Once we are born how do we satisfy our need for life?
There is a child in our arm
Is the child responsible for our impurities?
A child who has no knowledge of the Universe
Nature in its most innocent state
Purity and awareness?
The son of God is my idol?
Did Jesus die on a cross for my sins?
I believe he died on a cross of intoxication.

The Cup

There is a God who rules the world.
He never knew how much he was loved.

My God, my God,
        Why have you forsaken me?

Forsaken you, my dear friend.
They know not what they do.

The cup you desired
To be taken away
From your hand
In the Garden of Gethsemane,
I hand the cup back to you.

Who could forsake
Your level of awareness and, your purity?
My angel and friend,
Who could forsake you as their son?

Repetition

Repetitions are for our souls;
They are strangers in our hearts.

How does the mind become so hard?
It is chasing its own mind.
How did I become repetitive?

The truth of forgiveness
Is interesting for a reason:
It makes me wonder about how
To end a repetition.
How do I end repetitions?

I must forgive myself, too.

Love

Love itself is a question of rejection.
How does Love begin?
Comfort and fulfilment.

How did you find your mother's womb?
You never knew the natural world.
How did you find the voice of a father?
You didn't know the natural world.

There is a reason why rejection is so important:
It is for Nature to know why.

The bread expands,
The water becomes wine,
And you are born.
Rejection from the body is natural.

What happens to love?
Comfort and security takes its place;
Necessity and need become dominant.

The greater the distance from the origin,
The greater the need.

Natural Sign

There is distance we have to conquer.
How many times do you feel the need?
The need to find a home in your own mind—
The distance is love.

There is love inside the heart always;
It is a natural sign leading a way back home

Patterns

There are no parallels in our realm;
There are only patterns to chase
And patterns that dissolve
There is only quantum mechanics.

When I was a child I had a dream
That I would be among celestial beings

I am a human being.

Body Of Holiness

I am in need of your friendship,
In need of your heart.
I saw you as a human being,
A child uncloth'd.

How do you feel knowing my word is your heart?
Your beauty is my sin,
Your body my holiness.

Seeing Is, Believing

Love is real and for a reason:
In everything you see,
A second is without logic and reason.

How may I compare to you, knowing?
Feeling is everything in our realm.
Only now do I say

Seeing is, believing.

Altruism

I have no way of knowing
How to write down on my own.
I repeat myself until I stop;
I have dreamed about my soul.

How do we write down on our own
When so much of what we do
Involves the natural world

In my heart I feel altruism in all.
How may I say?

Forever and ever.

The Way Of Love

The way of love and peace is the power of the mind.
The great workable art is nature.
A planet is a solar system.
A solar system is a galaxy.
A galaxy is a universe.
A universe is a quantum reality.
The glory of the universal truth,
The way of love and order,

The way of love and peace.